Title: U.S. Military Fighter
R.L.: 3.7
PTS: 0.5
TST: 152253

D1607369

U.S. MILITARY FIGHTER PLANES

by Barbara Alpert

CONTENT CONSULTANT:
RAYMOND L. PUFFER, PHD
HISTORIAN, RET.
EDWARDS AIR FORCE BASE HISTORY OFFICE

READING CONSULTANT:
BARBARA J. FOX
READING SPECIALIST
PROFESSOR EMERITA
NORTH CAROLINA STATE UNIVERSITY

CAPSTONE PRESS
a capstone imprint

Blazers is published by Capstone Press,
1710 Roe Crest Drive, North Mankato, Minnesota 56003.
www.capstonepub.com

Library of Congress Cataloging-in-Publication Data
Alpert, Barbara.
    U.S. military fighter planes / by Barbara Alpert.
    p. cm. — (Capstone blazers: U.S. military technology)
    Includes index.
    Audience: Grades 4-6.
    Summary: Describes the fighter planes used by the U.S. military.
    ISBN 978-1-4296-8439-2 (library binding)
    ISBN 978-1-62065-210-7 (ebook PDF)
1. Fighter planes—United States—Juvenile literature. I. Title.
UG1242.F5A369 2013
623.74'640973—dc23

                                                    2012003592

Editorial Credits
Brenda Haugen, editor; Kyle Grenz, designer; Laura Manthe, production specialist

Photo Credits
DoD photo by Staff Sgt. Aaron Allmon, USAF, 14-15, Staff Sgt. Christopher Boitz, USAF, 24;
U.S. Air Force photo by Tech Sgt. Cohen A. Young, cover (top), Master Sgt. Adrian Cadiz, cover
(bottom), Airman 1st Class Brett Clashman, 9, Master Sgt. Jeremy Lock, 13, 26-27, Master Sgt.
William Greer, 5, 10-11, Staff Sgt. Andy M. Kin, 25, Staff Sgt. Jacob N. Bailey, 22-23, Staff Sgt.
Michael B. Keller, 17, 21; U.S. Navy photo by Cmdr. Erik Etz, 7 (bottom), MC1 Edward I Fagg,
18, MC1 Tommy Lamkin, 29 (bottom), MC3 Benjamin Crossley, 6-7; U.S. Navy photo courtesy of
Lockheed Martin, 29 (top)

Artistic Effects
deviantart.com/Salwiak, backgrounds

Printed in the United States of America in
Stevens Point, Wisconsin.
032012   006678WZF12

TABLE OF CONTENTS

THE SKY IS A BATTLEGROUND

What flies faster than a rocket blasting into space and higher than any other jets? A military fighter plane! These amazing jets battle enemy planes.

Fighter jets take off from huge **aircraft carriers** in war zones. These jets reach high speeds in short distances.

aircraft carrier—a large warship designed to carry and launch fighter planes

CHAPTER 1

DANGEROUS FIGHTERS

F-15E Strike Eagles track and attack enemy aircraft. They can turn without losing speed, making them hard to catch. F-15E Strike Eagles use radar to keep the enemy in sight.

FACT

Radar stands for "radio detection and ranging." Radar uses radio waves to figure out the distance, height, or speed of an object.

F-16 Fighting Falcons fly fast anywhere and in any weather. F-16 pilots can see in every direction from the **cockpit**. Powerful computers help locate targets at night and in bad weather.

cockpit

cockpit—the area in the front of a plane where the pilot sits

The Thunderbirds are a group of Air Force pilots who fly F-16s to show off amazing moves. They make loops, rolls, and tight turns while flying close together.

F-16 Fighting Falcon

CHAPTER 2

IT'S A DOGFIGHT!

F/A-18 Hornets fire big guns. These jets dive and roll to escape enemy gunfire. Hornets fly upside down to trick enemy pilots and win **dogfights**.

dogfight—a mid-air battle between fighter planes

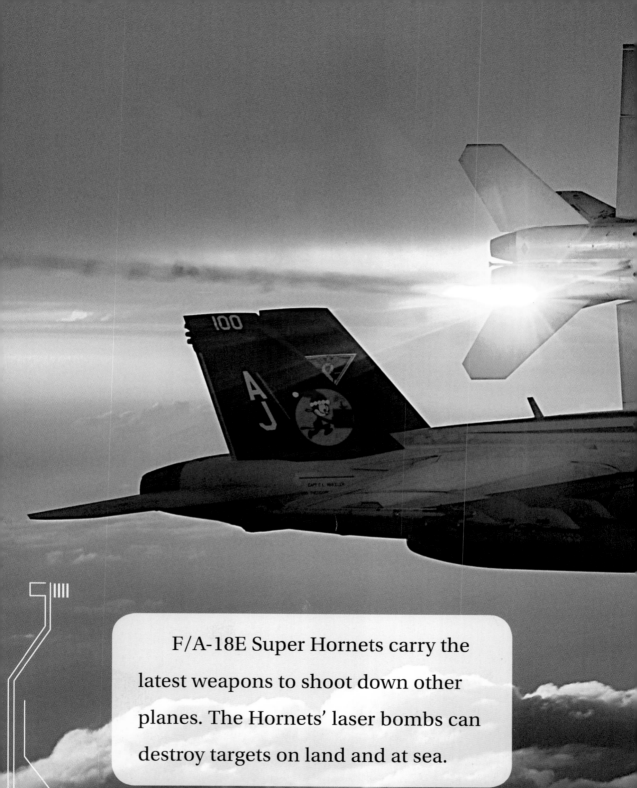

F/A-18E Super Hornets carry the latest weapons to shoot down other planes. The Hornets' laser bombs can destroy targets on land and at sea.

CHAPTER 3

QUICK AND DEADLY

The F-22 Raptor is the Air Force's newest fighter plane. Its engines use less fuel to fly farther than older jets.

FACT The Raptor flies at more than 1,500 miles (2,414 kilometers) per hour!

bay

The Raptor's **missiles** are kept in **bays**. The bays are hidden by the shape of the plane's wings. An enemy pilot can't see the Raptor's missiles until it's too late to escape.

missile—an explosive weapon that can travel long distances

bay—a compartment or space used for a special purpose

CHAPTER 4

CATCH ME IF YOU CAN

Fighter planes move in many ways. Pilots **maneuver** the jets to avoid getting shot. They fly in circles, straight up, straight down, and even upside down!

maneuver—to move in a planned and controlled way

A special paint on the wings makes it hard for enemies to see fighter planes on radar. Very thin wings also help keep fighter jets from being seen by enemies.

CHAPTER 5

HIGH-TECH ATTACK

The mission begins when a fighter pilot spots an enemy on a computer screen. Fighter pilots try to surprise an enemy by appearing suddenly and firing weapons.

The best Navy fighter pilots are trained in air combat. They go to the Navy Fighter Weapons School, also known as Top Gun. Tom Cruise starred in a movie of the same name.

Some U.S. fighter jets can climb up to 20,000 feet (6 km) in just over a minute.

The fastest fighter planes can fly 1,875 miles (3,017 km) per hour.

CHAPTER 6

TOMORROW'S FIGHTER PLANES

The F-35 Lightning II is called the fighter plane of the future. The Lightning II is hard to find and hard to hit. It's a super-fighter, and it's almost ready to go to work!

GLOSSARY

aircraft carrier (AYR-kraft KAYR-ee-uhr)—a large warship designed to carry and launch fighter planes

bay (BAY)—a compartment or space used for a special purpose

cockpit (KOK-pit)—the area in the front of a plane where the pilot sits

dogfight (DAWG-fite)—a mid-air battle between fighter planes

maneuver (muh-NOO-ver)—to move in a planned and controlled way

missile (MISS-uhl)—an explosive weapon that can travel long distances

READ MORE

Jackson, Kay. *Military Planes in Action.* Amazing Military Vehicles. New York: PowerKids Press, 2009.

Schmauss, Judy Kentor. *The World's Toughest Machines.* Extreme Machines. Chicago: Raintree, 2011.

Winchester, Jim. *Jet Fighters: Inside & Out.* Weapons of War. New York: Rosen Pub., 2012.

INTERNET SITES

FactHound offers a safe, fun way to find Internet sites related to this book. All of the sites on FactHound have been researched by our staff.

Here's all you do:

Visit *www.facthound.com*

Type in this code: 9781429684392

Super-cool stuff!

Check out projects, games and lots more at
www.capstonekids.com

INDEX